# Life Betwixt

Essays on Allies in the Everyday and Shamanism Among

## S. Kelley Harrell

Part of the Intentional Insights Blog-to-Book Series

Soul Intent Arts

Fuquay-Varina, North Carolina USA

Also by S. Kelley Harrell, from Soul Intent Arts

*Gift of the Dreamtime – Awakening to the Divinity of Trauma*

*Gift of the Dreamtime Reader's Companion*

*Real Wyrd – A Modern Shaman's Roots in the Middle World (Part of the Intentional Insights blog-to-book series)*

Books by S. Kelley Harrell available from Soul Rocks Books

*Teen Spirit Guide to Modern Shamanism – A Beginner's Map Charting an Ancient Path*

## Life Betwixt - Essays on Allies in the Everyday and Shamanism Among
by S. Kelley Harrell
© 2016

Cover Photo by Andreiuc88
Cover Design by S. Kelley Harrell

Published by Soul Intent Arts, LLC,
Fuquay Varina, NC 27526 US
info@soulintentarts.com
www.soulintentarts.com

ISBN 978-0-9860165-9-2
First printing May 2016
Printed in the United States of America
A Soul Intent Arts Publication

This book is available in print and as an ebook. Visit kelleyharrell.com to learn more about Kelley's writing, and soulintentarts.com for her blog and shamanic work.

## Dedication

To the teachers who have gone before,

the teachers who will come after,

and the teachers we never know have been.

## Acknowledgements

Thank you, readers of *Intentional Insights.* Because of your inquiries and interests in the modern shamanic path, my open dialogue with souls has become a thriving online collective presence, since 2004. That's elderhood in blogosphere years.

Always, thanks to Rob, Maya and Tristan, for being the sun, moon, and stars dancing in my world.

## Table of Contents

## Betwixt Introduction

In 2014, *Intentional Insights* celebrated ten years in the blogosphere. What began as a simple Q&A for readers to submit inquiries about modern shamanism, dreams, paranormal experiences, and spiritual healing, evolved into a dialogue of souls sharing the modern experience of animistic and shamanistic life.

It's been interesting for me to watch the overculture discussions of soulwork change in that time frame. When I began to work with others as a modern shaman in 1998, there was no cultural precedent for neither soul wounds, nor was there a working vocabulary for how to address them. Rare was it that someone sought me out with a request for soul retrieval, or even understood what soul loss was.

Now, just a few years later, not only do we have a framework for that dialogue, it's become a very mainstream part of our healthcare, media, and lifestyle awareness. That is truly a huge shift in a very short period of time.

In 2012, I published *Intentional Insights*' first blog-to-book, *Real Wyrd*, focused on my experiences as a lifelong intuitive and modern shaman experiencing things going bump in the night. Originally a series called "The Dead Time," on my blog, this book focuses on the lesser-emphasized spirituality of the immediate mundane, the Middle World, as it is referred to in triple cosmology dialogue. Few resources discuss the spiritual layer we have the most immediate access to, and when they do it's generally for entertainment or thrill-seeking purposes. *Real Wyrd* presents paranormal experiences and how as a shaman, I work within them to facilitate wellbeing. The book includes posts still on *Intentional Insights*, as well as original stories of the strange.

While the term 'shaman' is easily tossed around and the title stays under scrutiny, there is much about the lifestyle of shamanism in a modern context that seems to elude or perplex us. It remains fringe even in the most woo of circles.

In an effort to further extend that animistic reach into everyday life, I began writing another series on my blog called *Life Betwixt*. This series presents how to blend the sacred with the everyday, how to become a more active weaver of wyrd. It addresses some of the more common details of shamanistic life that fall through the cracks of classes on technique and ecstasy.

One of my biggest grievances of modern shamanism is that it's presented as a technique, rather than a lifestyle, a dilemma I addressed head-on in my book, *Teen Spirit Guide to Modern Shamanism*. With most modern shamanists predominantly emphasizing journeying and ecstatic trance over the role of shaman, a lack of insight and support for that role in contemporary life has created crisis for many. We don't talk about the support required to sustain the modern shaman. We don't talk about mental and emotional challenges of that role, and we often limit our understanding of just how taxing it is to have a foot in both worlds and still function in mundane society.

The hardest part of realizing the lifestyle of shamanism is that it truly is betwixt and between. It is neither fully one thing, nor the other. Our cultural doesn't reserve room for the liminal experience. We want well-defined boundaries with clear indications of what they are, of what stepping beyond them looks like, and how operating outside them impacts us. Once situated into the world of shamanism, there is no such concrete detail. There is only flux, and making peace with that fluid state of being is a requirement. Becoming flux is a requirement.

When we examine the definition of the phrase "betwixt and between" Dictionary.com cites it as "neither the one nor the other; in a middle or unresolved position." For a shaman, the liminal isn't just an unresolved position. It is an *unresolvable* position, with which peace must be made, over and over. We do not reconcile this role once, but ongoing.

Therein lies the biggest rub of the modern shamanism: community. In the twenty-five years of my study of shamanism, we still don't talk about the lifestyle around a shamanistic or animistic path, which frankly, has a lot to do with the problems that arise when learning to journey, sussing out personal relationship to concepts such as 'wounded healer' and 'hollow bone,' and the balance between personal wellbeing, community activism, and planetary responsibility.

This first installment of the *Life Betwixt* series intended to enlighten those on a shamanic path to greater allies, how to access them, and embody them throughout the day—not just when in trance. It emphasizes the relationship with local spirits (I call them home spirits) to create the foundation for community with spirit guides and human allies.

Despite its well-rooted presence in modern culture, shamanism is still new to our society. Who am I to bring insight on how to live it? Mostly, I'm someone who's noticed gaps in how we live it, and has taken on the challenge of open discourse about it to inform the seekers who will root it further.

How we shape the teaching and living of shamanism now will radically impact how the next wave of seekers teach, learn, live, and embody. In the spirit of such sharing, I leave my small contribution describing animism in the everyday, and shamanism among. To that end, join the Facebook community of the same name (Shamanism Among), and share your contribution to this evolution with a group of like-minded shamanists.

I am a lifelong intuitive, having focused my work into my shamanic practice, Soul Intent Arts since 2000. I am author of *Gift of the Dreamtime: Awakening to the Divinity of Trauma*, the *Gift of the Dreamtime Reader's Companion*, *Real Wyrd*, *Teen Spirit Guide to Modern Shamanism,* and I am vigorously involved with the worlds in and around me. My work focuses on grounding spiritual emergence into a healthy, balanced life between the mundane and magick. I teach classes on modern shamanism, as well as the two-year training, *The Spirited Path Intensive*, and the one-year training, *Reclaiming the Runes—Putting the 'Elder' Back in Futhark Intensive.* I hold private in-person and remote web conferencing sessions for Soul Readings, Shamanic Healing, and Chakra Balancing.

Some of the essays in this collection are revised from *Intentional Insights* posts, though several have never before been published.

## Chapter 1 - After the Journey

Then he began to think of all the things Christopher Robin would want to tell him when he came back from wherever he was going to, and how muddling it would be for a Bear of Very Little Brain to try and get them right in his mind. 'So, perhaps,' he said sadly to himself, 'Christopher Robin won't tell me anymore,' and he wondered if being a faithful Knight meant that you just went on being faithful without being told things.

~A. A. Milne, *The Wonderful World of Pooh*

I've always said there's no veil. There's no line that says here's Here, and—there's conveniently, separately located There, the official *Other Side*. Nonetheless, the need to articulate how that between experience feels and works in daily life requires some kind of identifier, and I'm not going to reinvent the conceptual wheel. Rather, I'll just go with what we've got.

So here's where this new direction starts: life after shamanic journeying. When I first discovered there were classes that taught shamanic techniques, that collection of exercises was put forward as the whole of shamanism. In short, they're not. What's even harder to process is that many teachers are still presenting journeying and shamanism in that synonymous way–as if merely the ability to slide into trance makes one a shaman.

Without celebration of our natural inclination toward trance states.

Without discussion of what to do with the information stirred by the mere process of journeying.

Without discussion of how life after that point changes–even in the absence of plans to become a shaman.

Without plans for how to carry the ecstatic experience into daily life–back to one foot in both worlds, healthily.

Without provisions for how to recreate that ecstasy on our own.

Many present the technique of journeying as the feature distinguishing shamanism from other intuitive/psychic arts. It is, though intentionally traveling into ecstasy isn't all that shamanism is. In fact, assuming the commonly accepted vernacular of journeying as "willing an aspect of the soul out of the body, to a specific spirit strata, to gain insight for wellbeing from spirit guides, which is manifest after returning to the body" isn't even the only way to make that trek— contrary to popular belief.

I've said from day one of deciding–and it is a decision–to accept my calling to be a modern shaman, that anyone can *see*. We're all seers, all intuitive. Going into trance doesn't make someone a shaman, it makes him or her human. It's not a special skill reserved for certain people.

However, knowing what to do with intuition, how to respond to it, how to incorporate its wisdom into everyday life is a very special skill, that can–and should–be learned, for our own journeys, and especially if for those of us who want to work with others. Otherwise, dipping into journeying can make a huge mess, a spiritual crisis bigger than what necessitated learning the technique to start with.

If realizing the role wrapping ecstatic trance is so important, why is it left out? The short answer is because it can't be taught in a weekend workshop, which is how most people learn of modern shamanism. It can't be taught from a book—not even one of my books. We make light of sacred teachings purported to have taken decades to master, suggesting that our lives move faster, our brains are more developed. The reality is, it takes time to seat a spiritual practice and animistic worldview amidst stress, paying bills, sustaining relationships, and processing the experiences of Other. And it always has. It's no different for modern seekers. There are no shortcuts. We don't know how to walk in both worlds without just doing it, and we do it best with support.

Honestly, I don't believe weekend woo teachers leave that information out on purpose. I believe many modern shamanists don't realize the damage done by putting shamanism out there so simply as 'just journey.' The teachers of the teachers don't know, so a legacy of not rooting a shamanic mind into an animistic life has generated a trail of ill-prepared shamanists.

To that end, a lot of people come to me after a crash weekend course in journeying, needing to sort it all out. Those two-day classes teach the skill, but they don't teach how to process what comes out of it. Intense group intimacy is created to generate the experience, yet how to create space sustained over time to support the blossoming of that work isn't taught. It can't be in such a short period of time. As a result, for many seekers, the experience ceases to grow beyond that class.

The thing is, it always grows beyond the class, the concern is whether we're capable of allowing and fostering that growth. There is no dabbling with shamanism. It changes us and demands that we step empowered into new perspective and direct relationship with All Things. When we can't do that, distress trumps the good things learned in the weekend class.

Apart from the emotional fallout–which spans absolute ecstasy to horror, depression to joy, and everything between–that often occurs after learning to journey, the thing I hear most from those who have started shamanistic classwork with another teacher is that they can't hold the ecstatic experience. They can't recreate it the way they felt it in those early soul adventures. The very first introductions we make, actively engaging the unseen, blow our socks off. Most definitely they alter our sense of self and Life, on a dime. Even people who consider their initial soul travels "unsuccessful," with regard to meeting allies recognize the innate power of the altered state. In fact, often those with least expectations are those most deeply affected. Without fail, though, eventually the colors fade, the messages obscure. Sometimes communication stops short, and guides don't even show up. Why?

Sure, part of that can be chalked up to dynamics. There's something magickal about group sacred space, particularly when it's created in a class based on the intention of facilitating and supporting soul travel. Creating space in isolation doesn't always get the same results. In fact, most intro to shamanism classes don't even emphasize the importance of or teach students how to create sacred space. However, done with the intention of bringing in the Nature Spirits of the familiar to help hold the space for soul travel, the journey can be even more personal, more secure, more transcendent.

Another culprit is not observing ritual for journeying. The key thing to know about not being able to sustain the thrilling, vivid journeys of fledgling soul travel is... no one can recreate it that first blissful way without manifesting through the rest of life what each journey teaches. We have to live what we learn in ecstasy in order for our mundane to support those travels. *Journeys become rote because shamanism isn't just journeying.*

Not being able to have lush soul travel on command isn't a personal fault; it's a deep divisive component of our individualistic culture. In the west, we aren't steeped in honoring the unseen through ordinary, commonplace gestures. Our standard mode of operation is one or the other–Here or There. We don't recognize both at once. Even those of us on devout religious paths generally aren't that thorough in bringing those spiritual tenets through all the days we're not in earshot of the congregation. We're not known for walking our talk. However, in the role of shaman, that lack of sightedness into the everyday will work against all well-intended ecstatic efforts very quickly. It will impact the ability to go into trance, and it will affect the quality of interactions that happen therein.

Without consistent observation of the unseen when we're not in trance, it's really hard to sustain exhilarating journeys into the Dreamtime. Journeying is all or nothing, in that to continue having life-altering experiences in trance, we have to manifest what we glean in them, in day-to-day life. What we do Here, directly impacts what we can achieve There. It's all connected. When we water our houseplants, we have to consider our relationship to them, how our care affects them, their choice in how they grow. When we walk through a space, we have to realize we aren't just moving through it, but are engaging with it. When we encounter conflict, we mustn't just rush to heal it, but consider its role in our story, consider its story. We can't just do the mental process of journeying, however ensouled we believe it to be. *We must embody our own ensouledness, and bring it through everything we do.*

As seekers on a shamanistic path it's not just suggested that we root into the unseen as deeply as possible, it's expected. We don't just roll up on the Other Side to learn things and heal ourselves or others. Relationships with Guides and Nature Spirits need reciprocity as much as other relationships in our lives. In fact, healing can't happen unless we invest in those relationships. Healing happens because of those relationships.

And for the record, shamanic journeying isn't just the vehicle allowing us to form relationships to the spiritual allies we encounter in that state, it's a relationship to journeying, itself.

*Journeying is a lifestyle change.* It gives us the seeds to grow what we need in our lives. Unplanted, nothing can grow, Here or There. Planted, we grow everywhere.

Consider personal relationship to journeying. What parts of it work? What parts of it don't support personal needs and expectations?

Consider how to root the insights of journeying into the everyday. Is it possible? What might have to change for it to become possible?

In the next time journey, widen the senses, and focus awareness on a sense that isn't usually engaged when traveling out. Perhaps don't focus on any sense at all, and see what comes. Indeed, the soul navigates the trip, though the mind and body filter it into useful data. How does the clarity and retention of that data shift when filtered through other senses?

## Chapter Two - Working with Home Spirits

*Wherever you stand, be the soul of that place.*
*~Rumi*

It all starts here, or more specifically, it starts at home. So often the conversation of beginner shamanism opens with talk of spirit guides, helping spirits, totems, deities–which are all well and good. However, when we begin to stretch into far strata, we often forget about allies in our backyard. There are other influential souls with whom we can enter into deep relationship, and they're right under our noses, every day. I call them my Home Spirits, though they are referred to many ways.

These are the Nature Spirits, wights, land elders, and the consciousness of my actual home–the dwelling in which I live–who are guardians with whom I am in relationship all the time. We all have them, and they are unique not only to our home and location, but to each person living in our space. They may be the favorite hellebores in the side garden, the cactus in a planter by the front door, the lawn, itself. They may be souls of indigenous land keepers, elementals that have never been in form, the spiritual manifestation of the town, city, or bioregion. The soul of our home, each room, every beam, can engage us, and we should absolutely engage them. These beings comprise our first tribe, and the one most readily available to us.

Again, if the relationship to the spiritual Nature right in front of us is so important, why isn't it taught *before* all the Guide and totem hoopla? Partly because humans have a tendency to think the grass is always greener elsewhere—literally. The New Age culture has brought us spiritual tourism, the ability to find enlightenment in cultures, regions, and rituals deemed more spiritual than our own. As a result, we have created a sort of manufactured authenticity, what I call 'croissan'wich sacredness.' This combination of appropriating spirituality from other cultures and trying to situate it into western landscapes and lifestyles separates us from the spirituality of the ley we're already on.

Likewise, the New Age has given us complexes about who our Nature Spirits and totems are, as well as projections about who they should be. The phrase 'Big Impressive North American Birds and Mammals' (BINABM) has come to describe the bias conveyed and perceived in working with animal allies.

Journeying, itself can be used to create division, as well. It's not called 'journeying' that for no reason. We leave the familiar landscape of our bodies to venture into strata beyond imagination. Many of us are quite comfortable with the ecstasy of trance, to stay in awe of Spirit Teachers and hold them at noble distance. However, we struggle to embody them and live as fully in concert with them as the role of shaman requires. In that sense, journeying can be escapist and create distance, rather than close it.

It's easier to think shamanic life is a novelty meant to savored as a treat, than it is to realize it's a 24/7 commitment to being. And frankly, it's easier to teach it that way, too. It's much easier to teach a skill such as journeying and set students on their ecstatic way, than it is to hold the portal open to mentor them through what's on the other side, and the *other* other side, and integrate it all, ongoing We sit most comfortably with spiritual life as something that we do at interval, like vacation or retreat, rather than breathing it throughout everything we do. That lack manifests most evidently in the disconnect between ourselves and the immediate space we inhabit.

Another reason modern shamanists don't engage Home Spirits is that the teachings we were given made us afraid of the Middle World, as it is called in a triple cosmology. Known in many cosmologies by many names, the Earth's soul, the spiritual layer of everything on the planet, the space of dreams, and many other things, our most immediate connection to all things spiritual has become demonized. Many believe it's the most dangerous space to traverse because it's not exclusively our own. It can be a space of restless grief, fear, and suffering from humanity. It can be a space filled with joy and powerful blessing. It holds what we as a human collective have put there, and vast other wisdom from every other inhabitant and caregiver of Earth, for all of its time. My conclusion for why this layer is hardest for us to engage, why it's been held separate in most modern studies, is that we're the most emotionally connected to the Middle World. As such, we have a harder time detaching from its inhabitants and experiences.

*Which doesn't mean we shouldn't try.*

*Which doesn't mean we aren't capable.*

*Which doesn't mean we aren't still responsible for its wellbeing.*

Being aware of spaces and how we use them, move through them, contribute to them, are affected by them, affect them–all of these are important. Despite that we use them *for* spiritual practice, most of us don't bring them *into* our personal spiritual practice. We're more conscientious of the rituals we do in spaces, the fetishes brought into them, the altars we build in them. Yet, how often do we actually engage the spirits of our home space? How often do we enquire about the needs of the land's elders? How do they embrace (or not) other cultural flavors/allies of our spiritual path?

We don't blossom where we imagine we are. Rather, *we can only prosper where we are.* We must be fully present at home, in order to be grounded to travel elsewhere. When we live in spiritual concert with the Home

Spirits, every being in that rapport is blessed. Family becomes a much bigger concept. Care and tending of the land and creatures who live on it become needed rituals far beyond just living green and sustainable permaculture. We become responsible for each other. We engage in reciprocity at a grassroots level.

Acknowledge Home Spirits, first of all. Honor what they have contributed to the household, and how they continue to. Create an opening to interact with them. Get a feel for what beings are ever-present in the home space. Invite them into etheric space and communicate with them. Are they ones already engaged in spiritual matters, or are they new? How are they connected to the land, the home? How do they want to connect? Ask what they need. State what is needed from them.

This ongoing dialogue is key to being fully present in an animistic life, certainly in fulfilling the role of shaman. Historically, shamans served the tribe, which was framed in a particular territory. Their relationship with the Nature Spirits of that terrain enabled their success at caring for their tribe, at growing into their skills, and in working with other shamans, other terrains. It also preserved their boundaries, giving a natural guideline not to overextend.

We don't all have the same access to Nature. Some live in city flats, others on farms, carefully manicured suburbia–none of which really matters when we consider the uniqueness of the relationships we form with and around our personal space.

For that matter, some of us aren't that enthused about direct interface with Nature. Sit with that contradiction, truly. Honestly open up to the personal role in working with local spirits, and what they need. No one has to suddenly become a gardener, wilderness enthusiast, or master of sacred space. But we do each have to become the master of *our* sacred space, or at least its willing host to be part of its mastery of being, of relating. These spirits are the eyes and ears of the places in our lives that we can't attend. They are the true guardians of our homes, our personal domains. We are a manifestation of theirs.

I work with many clients who despise working with people. They feel the toll a lack of spiritual community has taken in their lives, yet they have been hurt enough that they refuse to reach out to humans for support. I remind them that Nature is the First Tribe. We are all born animists. We are all born enamoured with some facet of Nature, whether it's climbing trees, picking lovely flowers, or having a best animal friend. Remembering that first sip of animism can go along way to quenching spiritual thirst in adulthood. Being able to reconnect with that childhood bond is critical to gaining and giving support to the Home Spirits. When we do that, humans who do the same show up in our lives. Human interconnection becomes easier.

When I first started working with the Home Spirits of our current residence, I was greeted by many. They told me that in order for the balance between the physical and spiritual world to sustain and evolve, every place that hosts humans must have a human conduit into the spirit world. According to them, every human haunt demands a shaman. Their remark wasn't about human-centricity, so much as we are animals in their space. All beings sharing space must find a way to form community and engage life together. There must be a sentient bridge through which an exchange of life force happens, a consolidated awareness is forged, and all involved benefit. This wasn't put to me as a suggestion for every square inch of the entire planet, but a requirement for those that sustain humans, are affected by humans. We're supposed to be engaged with the spirits of our home.

One of the best ways to engage them is through the Land Elders. They are humans who lived on the land, who through life and at the point of death elected to guard it, to be the spiritual liaison for the humans who would come later.

We are those newcomers.

Ask the Elders of the land if it's appropriate to merge, so that their wisdom can be available to its humans. Ask how they overcame feelings of separation, community dissent toward Nature, and/or how they carried the mantle of being the human soul ambassador to the land. Ask them how to hold the space for the land, to meet the needs of our time.

Allied with the Land Elders, greet all the Home Spirits—the fae, the wights, the plants, animals, trees, mineral, elements, the residence—as many as are willing.

We can't deeply root into our own gifts and fulfill our needs until we connect with the spirits most immediately around us. They're viable. They are important to our personal path, and our relationship with them is vital to the collective path of the planet. They are the roots we so often try to find in ourselves, forgetting they were already there.

Invoke them.

Bless them.

Thank them.

Serve them.

Be them.

Working with Home spirits isn't just about where we're located. It's about where we're going, where they've been, and carrying out our role in getting the planet where it needs to be.

## Chapter Three - Reciprocity with Spirit Guides

Spirit Guides are sometimes called angelic guardians, allies, or Spirit Teachers. They may even be split into roles, such as helper—one who comes to assist through a specific life phase or task, or as is more commonly noted the "Guide," a helper who stays with us for the long haul of this life, maybe for many. They may also be allies handed down to us through ancestry.

We also have what some refer to as animal guides, totems, medicine spirits. These are complex beings who represent aspects of the natural world, bringing us their skills and wisdom, protection, awareness. Some use the term 'totem' generically, referring to any animal guide that comes, while for others, it refers to a guiding Nature Spirit that has been in the tribal or family line for ages, such that not only are the traits and wisdom of that totem handed down, so is the relationship, itself. Refer to my book, *Teen Spirit Guide to Modern Shamanism* for a more in-depth exploration of Guides and Nature Spirits, and how we can engage them.

Most people use the generic phrase, "animal guide" to refer to the spirits of the natural world. As I work almost exclusively with plant and elemental spirits, I call them Nature Spirits, to honor that any being of the natural world can become an ally. Whatever we call them and however they are active in our lives, a concept that comes up often in circles of traditional shamanism is that of reciprocity with spirit allies, or what some refer to as 'the demands of their Guides. I've known shamans whose Guides required them to make all of their ritual items. Nothing could be store-bought or given by another. Some are required to dedicate one day a week to cut off communication and engagement with others, and for that day live in concert only with a specific guide. Leaving a place setting for the Guide at every meal is mandatory for some. Body modification may be a condition of connecting with a Guide. Others are required to wear talismans of a particular totem, such as feathers, fur, or skin of that totem.

In traditional shamanism, such demands are business as usual. The Baule people in the Ivory Coast in West Africa have spirit spouses, for whom one night of the week is set aside to honor that relationship and in some cases, placate issues in it. The weekly step into the Dreamtime relationship brings healing and awareness that often is choked in human partnerships. Buryat hunters must apologize to their kills and end the lives of their game in a specific way, in order to uphold the balance of Nature.

For people who don't bring their spirit relationships into their daily life, these seem like extreme examples of reciprocity. Within the respective cultural frameworks, these supernatural observances are a natural function of daily life.

In the modern context, the concept of demanding Guides is a somewhat off-putting idea, that in order to have their full support, we need to comply with certain wishes, on their part. Generally speaking, we don't live in an animistic society. We can't get away with hugging trees, let alone expressing devotion to one, passion to a guardian deity, or just responsibility for the spiritual or literal wellbeing of a bioregion.

Likewise, we're not monastic. We aren't in a culture that by virtue of a spiritual calling can set ourselves aside from cluttered, busy life while we develop that relationship. Most of us don't cloister ourselves for even short periods of retreat, as a means of growing, refining, and maintaining raw connection with the Divine, let alone remove ourselves completely. We find the sacred amidst work, bills, and everything else that has to be done.

Despite this distinction from traditional shamanism, judging the imperative of ally reciprocity as archaic is a very capitalist way to look at the give-and-take nature that should underlie every relationship in our lives. Balanced exchange is no different with Guides. Despite our best strides in incorporating a shamanistic worldview, we still look upon such bare demands as archaic, or out-moded. By our keen intellect and assumed civilized evolution, we see ourselves as somehow beyond that base need.

As a result, reciprocal relationship with Guides isn't taught in most contemporary shamanic coursework, despite that there are significant spiritual needs that it fills, and very mundane ones, as well. Most teachers approach Guides as omniscient resources set above humans, who function at the discretion of the shaman, rather than a mutual partnership focused on the wellbeing of All. Guides are noted as there to heal, serve, and teach. No one ever questions the needs of a Spirit Guide.

Foremost, demands from Spirit Guides, aren't as rudimentary as "Do this, or no dice." That simplistic way of looking at reciprocity brings to mind the pervasive idea that once called to a shamanic path, we have no choice but to follow, that we surrender free will. Often referred to as 'fire in the head,' for many shamanic students such mental ferocity is daunting–the state of being spiritually awakened and unable to dismiss that fact, to return to life as it was before.

It should be daunting, though not because it's fearsome, but because *it demands that we change*, and that demand often comes in the form of our Spirit Guides setting a few ground rules. Once that hollow bone circuitry gets opened up, we're in uncharted territory. We need a few easy-to-follow guidelines to keep us in check, but to also hold us steady in the life changes that come. In that light, the demands of Spirit Guides aren't about kissing the sacred ring, but having parameters set for our spiritual safety that we don't know how to set for ourselves. Honoring the demands of Spirit Guides is one way to accomplish that, in a very brass tacks, chop-wood/carry-water approach. Getting our hand dirty in the mundane requests of our Guides helps us to sustain the ecstasy through the rest of life, and stay sane.

Still, there's more going on than quickening the mouse in the transpersonal maze. Another component of placating Guides is the subtler demand that we go deeper within ourselves, into spiritual being. The requests of Guides are at heart designed to keep us on track when we're not communing with them in trance, specifically in ways that we would not otherwise monitor ourselves. Keep in mind, we're not all driven by the same challenges. *We are only affected by what's in our context, so the challenges we're given match that strata.* For an advertising executive on a shamanic path, being asked to honor intuition over sales and stats may be as challenging as building an ark. For a staunch herbalist, being told to rely on the spirit of allopathic healing could incite crisis. Maybe we're not asked to avoid all plastic, or make our own drums, or grow our ritual herbs. That omission doesn't mean there isn't a need and way to go deeper with our Guides.

The onus to learn if we need such may fall on us to ask.

A complication to reciprocity with Guides comes in the jaunt to collect them like trophies. I encounter many budding shamanists who value quantity over quality, when it comes to working with Spirit Guides. We need what we need; however, when those Allies begin to voice needs, juggling several can be distressing. There is a tendency to invite a distinct Guide (also, totem, fetish) for every life nuance and need. For instance, some people call in Guides to help with a specific relationship, or to provide insight into a specific chakra, or to preside over a particular habit. There isn't anything wrong with this approach, per se, though considering how many intimate relationships we can sustain at any one time applies to working with Guides, as much as in connecting with humans. Some people can juggle a lot of Allies and manage to stay in close, embodied relationship with all of them, or at least sustain the commitment agreed upon for that interaction. Many, though, cannot, and the result is etheric clutter. Instead of taking a few Guide relationships deeper they amass a menagerie of spiritual leadership, which can lead to conflicting directives, a lack of bonding needed to sustain life between trances, and the inability to establish meaningful reciprocity.

Our Soul Allies light the fire in those initial visits, but it's up to us to keep it burning. We have to ask our Guides and Nature Allies how to take our relationship with them deeper, and actually do that work. We must honor their demands of us to maintain our earthly connection to them, to our own spirit throughout mundane life. In that reciprocated connection, the mundane isn't so mundane.

Visit primary Guides, and clarify what work should be at the fore. Clarify with whom it should be done. Along with that line, ask the needs of Guides and comply. Learn how to honor them throughout the day, by becoming invested in meeting their needs.

With them, always consider how best to honor connection with them throughout the day, and what we can give back.

It really does take both to fully embody working with Guides.

## Chapter Four - Life Between Journeys

In the twenty-plus years that I took classes on various shamanic approaches, I never once heard anyone utter the words "life between journeys." So, now I make sure to say them constantly.

I've discussed how shamanism is presented as if journeying is the sum experience of shamanizing, and how the lack of learning or even becoming aware of the role of shaman incites crisis for many beginners. Another component of divine impatience relevant to the general modern spiritual community, not just shamanists, is the need to let wisdom rise.

The fluffy, happy culture of feel better/do good has created a relentless drive to constantly chase enlightenment. There's nothing wrong with seeking spiritual insight, except that it's exhausting to do constantly, and is also pointless. Seeking that affirmation of clarity and ecstasy of awe creates a deficit of stamina to actually do just that, because finding those treasures is only half the equation. We must learn how to sustain them and draw wisdom from them, ongoing. As long as we string out the ecstasy of awe, we won't do the work required to mine its precious teachings.

We *can* be more active in that passive learning. We're *capable* of doing it, yet human nature is led by the dangling carrot. We love spiritual AHA! Moments, though not so much the downtime between them, the time it takes for them to internalize and create the solid foundation for What Comes Next.

Years ago I complained to my mentor about my day job, which I badly wanted out of and felt utterly trapped in. She told me without hesitation that I would never get out of that job until I loved it. Upon hearing the words I was furious, sickened, even.

I couldn't imagine ever loving that job. I didn't hate it, so much as I felt confined in my life somewhat because of it. Yet I bought into her words, because she knew best, right?

I went on to read loads of New Age wisdom on being stuck, how it's our own fault, it's the result of unhealed wounds, it's a lack of imagination, a lack of realizing we create our own reality.

I turned to the shamanic community, which reinforced the unhealed wounds dogma, and told me to journey more about it. It encouraged soul retrieval, indicating that for me to become unstuck, I must have all of me here, now, integrated into my earthly consciousness.

So I did it, all. I returned all kinds of soul parts who brought back wonderful, healing wisdom. I devoted time every day to loving my day job by expressing genuine gratitude to it for all that it provided me and my family. I brought my spiritual practices into the workplace, and began working with the Office Spirits, there. I put into mundane practice the rites and healing received from ecstasy.

For weeks, my mentoring sessions were dominated with the mantra "Chop wood, carry water," and how through the drudgery of silent repetition, the divine is found in the most mundane of tasks. I undertook every boring daily task, like washing dishes, pulling weeds, and brushing my teeth, as a sacred act, an opportunity to find Divinity in the mundane.

I did it all until I was worn out, and nothing in my circumstances changed. While the work had served me in supportive humbling ways, it mostly served to make me aware of my depth for masochism—even that which was spiritually motivated to heal.

I freaked out, cried a lot, and stopped doing all of the work, save engaging the Nature Spirits of Home and my workplace. I wanted connection with them, because those relationships brought the most support to my life concerns. Instead of projecting a generalized idea of where I should be on my path and how I should be doing, they met me where I was and offered personal insights intended only for me. They reminded me through my own patterns and history that I can't flit back and forth between the unseen and the seen. I must be rooted in each, *all the time*. I must realize *they are never separate*. Everything I do in one *impacts the other*.

And that was when the wisdom came through. I didn't have to love my day job, but I did have to bless it. I had to find spiritual value in it, which as an animist, is a potent currency I can never say no to.

The truth is, even the most dull tasks fill spiritual needs, if we let them. They feed us, clothe us, keep the lights on, which are all pretty powerful energetic exchanges. And in hindsight, it's pretty lazy to assume that ecstasy will be served up any time it's desired. If we had access to spiritual bliss at any drop of a hat, we'd stay so frozen in the enjoyment of that moment that we'd be constantly vulnerable to the fear of it leaving. It would become a PTSD all its own. We must take up the onus of sustaining it in our own personal way, and come into deep direct understand of what that way is.

When we know our way and engage it regularly, we come into relationship with the patience to give it time and space to grow.

The best things we can ever do to deepen our journey experiences is to step back, take deep breaths, get off our own cases, and connect with a tribe that supports us in doing just that.

Make the effort. Invest more in the everyday. Find that tribe, and realize self is as spiritual in the everyday as in ecstasy.

## Chapter Five - The Guidance Within

Just as we don't often emphasize life between journeys as significant to the soul's growth, a topic often overlooked in many esoteric arts circles as well as in modern shamanism is personal truth, or as it is more commonly called is Unverified Personal Gnosis (UPG).

Most of us come from religious paths that strictly forbad us to act as our own spiritual conduit with the Divine. Part of what leads us to a more direct path is realizing the lack in such spiritual tropes. Yet, I see this same trap wrapped in different words and habits in esoteric arts all the time. I've known people who won't order food from a menu without asking their Guide's input, first. I've known others who firmly believe that a ritual to Air won't evoke the favor of the element if it isn't done precisely so, every time. I've known intuitives who were called upon to assist in emergencies but declined because they didn't have their portable altar with them to create sacred space. I've known people who never once uttered an insight of their own, replying "Well, my Guides say ___," or "I can't comment until I ask Mama Brown Bear."

How we roll with our Spiritual Council is exactly that–our relationship with our personal Spirit Allies. Part of the shaman-Guide relationship is knowing its boundaries, with regard to spiritual discipline, and possibly even personal wellbeing. I've got my own sacred eccentricities, which unmonitored lead to rote rituals and rigid perceptions. I've had plenty of times that disciplined, methodical practice—however artful and lovely—left me static in my process. For instance, drumming stopped working for me years ago as a method of induction to ecstatic trance. But all shamans drum! I'm supposed to drum! No. It quit working for me. Once I accepted that, yet again I didn't jive with the norm taught to me and let go of the projection, better methods revealed themselves.

Above all else on my path, I'm an advocate of results and growth, and I find that when I inhibit my instinctive responses, I stop getting meaningful results from my actions, however blessed and well-intended.

We're creatures of habit, and the one thing that focused, dedicated journeying will teach in a hurry is dynamic self-reliance. Yes, the core component of a shaman's effectiveness is committed relationship to Spirit Allies, though that doesn't mean to the effacement of self. *The idea that we sacrifice our innate wisdom at the feet of our Guides is really no different from the rigid religious doctrines that talked us out of our childhood spiritual knowing.*

Soul Allies don't want to be a crutch or habit. They don't want to be a convenient escape, or to keep circling the same healing wagons with us. In fact, projecting that wisdom can *only* come from Guides eventually strains our relationship with them. When we stop forcing their counsel out of habit, the emphasis on belief that we need to do so ceases, and a willingness to enable direct experience with personal truth emerges. There can and should be a fine balance of both.

Our Guides want and need us not to just explore and implement UPG, but to stand in it. Not once, but over and over. This edict doesn't mean force our truth on other people, or insist that our UPG trumps known science, possibly history. It means hold it alongside what is known and widely accepted, *for ourselves.* That's the thing about truth. Even if core truths we knew of ourselves at the age of four are still true at age fifty, the ability to hold ourselves open to the possibility that they can change creates the evolving atmosphere for them to remain true.

Years ago, a dear friend summed it best: "We find truth, we know it, then we set it down, and back gently away."

We must make peace with the demand to become active participants in our own Spiritual Council. However uncomfortable we find the idea of being 'wise,' or 'aware,' part of our job in self-healing is defusing the ego charge of these concepts. That charge runs the gamut of not believing that we can be wise, to believing we don't have the right to be, and fear of being misled by our truth. We forget that the body has its own wisdom. Soul components of ourselves can make meaningful contributions to our spiritual path and practice. *We are wise.* When we realize that fact, our shamanic path verges from self-centric healing, to collective healing and advocacy.

Given that, how do we discern UPG from the insight of our Guides? Do we even have to? How much does ascribing the source of insight matter, as long as it rings true? These are individual considerations with which we all must find balance. I don't always know precisely where an insight came from. I do hear my Guides' different voices, along with that of higher aspects of myself, my body, an individual organ, the grass. For me, what it comes down to is having developed a keen ability to pin-point my truth, and actually listen to it, act on it when I hear it. In the end, I don't care where it came from. I'm just glad I could receive it.

When we can accept our personal truths, our life view shifts from the divisions of Here and There, to the moment, to no veil, to All Things. The power of Spirit Teachers doesn't weaken when we initiate ourselves as Allies. If anything, it strengthens.

Ask the hard questions about personal truth. If the concept feels foreign, remember that all things are souls and can be communicated with. Ask the spiritual manifestation of personal truth to enter into journey space, and get to know it. This may be what some call the High Self, True Self, or GodSelf. It doesn't really matter what it's called, as long as the connection is there. Learn what it needs, and how it can be manifest through everyday life.

Delve into personal truth. Our Guides can take it.

## Chapter Six - The Sacred I Don't Know

In keeping with the examination on how we derive higher guidance regarding reciprocity with Guides, to take the next step in our guidance it's appropriate to reflect on a more intangible source of guidance: Everything.

Seems that one would be pretty obvious, since everything is around us all the time. Despite identifying as animists, most of us don't regard what's right in front of us as being Divine. Alive, maybe; aware, probably. Considering everything around us as Divine can be a very challenging practice to sustain through the day.

For me that momentum took shape by taking time daily to connect with the spirits of my space, wherever I was—at work, home, the grocery store, the homes of others, and the commute connecting it all. It seems so silly. I've spent all these years focused on *this* Nature Spirit, *that* guide, *this* space, sacred on/off, etc., despite that intellectually I've known it's with me all the time.

*I am it.*

*It is All.*

What's the expression–stick with the hell we know–to say nothing of the sacred.

Take a minute to consider ritual tools. Did they give their permission to be used? Were they even asked if they wanted to be used?

Every fetish we incorporate into ritual is a being that deserves to be honored—drums, rattles, crystals, altar cloths, bones, divination tools. Our work must weave its essence through what we do. When we expand that awareness to what we wear, what we eat, the opportunity to connect with everything around us—particularly items we engage with purpose—enriches everything we do.

As I implemented that practice, I sat more comfortably with not having to name everything, or delineate its rank in my spiritual council. I found deeper relationships–even if they only last a few moments. The realization that whatever I need is wherever I am, *all the time, no matter what*, was heady empowerment. It was also terribly humbling.

One thing I tell students, Initiates, and clients all the time is there's only one trick to the currently practiced technique or path being explored, and that's *remembering to do it*. Pause for a split second, step out of the routine, and remember the goal. Change the routine. Behave differently. *The secret to successful animism and shamanism is remembering to engage, at every opportunity.* How hard that can be to implement in everyday life!

There's another thing, though, that's just as important, and that's forgiving self upon realizing the tendency to make things hard.

Forgive self for forgetting and in very the next moment, remember, engage.

Discern the need of the moment. Take the time to ask and allow whatever life force in the immediate space can help meet that need. Bring it in on the breath. It's not necessary to know what it is, how it works, what it does. Just ask and allow it. Let it do its thing. Let the allies of the immediate external space bring a better internal place. Intend it on the breath for a couple of minutes, then re-asses the need. What feels different? What shifted? How does that shift settle into the body?

In that allowance, consider what can be given back, what exchange of life force can be made. Thanks? A blessing of some sort? A song or dance?

The body is many things, the least of which is how we engage formed being. It is the vessel through which we divine All Things. Let it.

## Chapter Seven - Working with Ancestor Allies

We've established the significance of Home Spirits, Spirit Guides, and our innate Higher Self. We've talked about the possible significance of every spiritual ally that assists us along our path. Just as important is focusing on the ancestors, and in doing so, realizing that in the western world working with them is a bit different than in indigenous cultures.

Modern shamanism has made art of connecting with Spirit Guides and Nature Spirits. The terminology, as well as techniques for finding them, are very commonplace in esoteric circles, now. However, very little emphasis is given to ancestors—those of our family line who have lived fully, persevered through the experience of the form, then moved on to anchor the wisdom of that formed experience into guidance for their earthly successors.

Keep in mind, the understanding of 'ancestor' can have great range. It may refer to someone in the blood family line. It may refer to a being from another plane, a Nature Spirit in the cellular or etheric nexus, a far-flung rock in space, or a relative from another manifestation of self. Regardless of the connection to ancestors, when we in the west talk about working with them, generally a great deal of healing must come first.

Why?

Because we don't look back.

Because we are a broken path.

Because we have hundreds of years of backlogged unhealed crap from those who came before us, and it has to manifest somewhere.

It's ironic that so much of healing and psychotherapy is given to dealing with our personal past, with little to no thought given to the etheric plight of our family line or collective past. As surely as we sustain personal hurts, so does our collective life force. Because we don't extend our awareness of the collective self backward, we don't direct healing in the rearview, either. Ultimately, that lack of healing stunts just how much we can accomplish in personal wellbeing, or in bringing wellness to our present family and communities.

In shamanistic cultures, emphasis on dying well is directly impacted by how one lives, which is to say, people who live with an eye toward the unseen, die without as much (or any?) baggage. They tend not to take the unresolved affairs of life into their deathwalk. What our ancestors heal of their lives, we, the living, don't have to carry. Of course this is a very simplified view and by no means categorical.

Regardless of culture, people engaging a foot in both worlds tend not to sit on trauma. Their soul retrievals are done immediately after wounding, and there is tribal understanding and support of healing; thus, they don't carry etheric scars into the afterlife. As a result, healing doesn't have to be done after death, to ensure that they move on to their destiny healthily, that they have the option to be empowered ancestral allies.

Western culture doesn't generally embrace living with an eye toward preparing the consciousness for death. We avoid discussion of dying, the afterlife, and how thoughts, beliefs, and actions affect both. As a result, we are more likely to experience soul loss that sustains over a long period of time, creating post-traumatic stress disorder (PTSD), which isn't resolved prior to death.

As animists, we know that unhealed wounds take on a life force of their own. They become golems, or my understanding of true daemons, that don't just vanish when the soul leaves the body. That life force has to go somewhere. These dynamics linger and must be picked up by the collective consciousness (ie, to all of us), to the restless (haunted) consciousness of the deceased, and to living loved ones. They most often transfer to those nearest or closest to them, and the living have no idea the transaction occurred. Our wounds in death are carried on, in the formed experience of our successors. Clearly this has significant potential to impact family lines. Thinking in terms of mass killings, wars, epidemics, the impact unhealed ancestors have on the collective conscious is enormous. Such are ancestral leftovers we all carry.

As our culture doesn't readily teach skills to release the drama of our own lives, it scarcely embraces the concept of amassed trauma passed to us from our ancestors, let alone how to heal it. Because of this, in order to work with our ancestors as allies, we first have to ensure their wellbeing.

There pervades the assumption that because a human has crossed into non-form, its soul is suddenly healed and wise, that the state of being without form imparts skills in wellbeing and leadership. In my experience as a deathwalker, not only is that not true, it's a dangerous assumption. Before we can turn to ancestors for wisdom, we must heal the troubled legacy they have left at our feet.

How do we know when we have an unhealed ancestral legacy? A big indicator that I frequently explore with students and clients is the lack of movement on a needed life change. When a place in life is identified as needing healing—change—and all appropriate resources are poured into it to no avail, the wound doesn't reside with that individual. That wound came before the individual, or was picked up from some other unhealed source. Every gesture we do to better ourselves and life around us evokes change, however minute. It may be an improved emotional space, relief of physical symptoms, a shift in a relationship. It may be the improved effectiveness of a coping skill. However it manifests, change is evident, even if subtle. So when we give a troubling dynamic everything we have and feel no movement, it's likely because the source of that imbalance doesn't lie with us. It could stretch to sources other than ancestors (living loved ones, a regional upset, etc), though ancestors are the place I look first. Despite that the source doesn't stem from us, healing can still be accomplished by us.

For some that healing can be easily done. For others, it may be more involved, and require the help of someone who sees the dynamic more objectively. Healing ancestors doesn't require being a shaman. It doesn't require skilled intuitive abilities. What is needed is an open heart, and the ability to focus the highest energy possible onto the souls who need it.

This kind of release work can be done purely to bless any disempowerment held onto by ancestors–physical, emotional, psychological, or spiritual–so that we, in turn are free of these dynamics, as well. However best suits personal spiritual practice, in a quiet space call in spiritual allies. Trust that they respond.

Express to them the intention that they heal ancestors in need.

Sit with that interaction, and note any sensations, thoughts, memories.

Sing to the ancestors. Express empathy for their life experience, and support for their healing of it. Express the desire to embody their wisdom, and connected interest in guiding loved ones who follow. There is no need to relive their experience for it to release. Honor any shadow components that come up. Defer to Guides to monitor the interaction, and show self and all involved abiding compassion.

Allow Spirit Allies to do whatever healing work is appropriate for the ancestors, for self, and for any life force between that is shared. If necessary, bring that healing forward into other family members, later generations, earlier generations. Along the ancestral line, there is no such thing as time. Allow the healing of it all, as much as can be done at this time, along every branch of the family tree, for all time.

When that work is done, allow it to move through the body. Again, note any sensations, thoughts, memories, or awareness that comes.

Thank the ancestors.

Thank Spirit Guides.

Thank self.

If honoring the ancestors and their plight in that way doesn't bring relief of some discontent, do seek out a shaman who can assist in bringing healing through the ancestral line. When we give attention to releasing the suffering of those who came before us, we clear the space more appropriately to address our own. Healing them doesn't mean that we're suddenly free of all affliction. It means that what afflictions we are faced with are ours, and not the result of thousands of years of amassed trauma. From helping our ancestors shift from suffering into release, we gain allies in the work our own lives require. We become ready to realize that relationship and embrace the insight of our lineage.

Know that in taking responsibility for the healing of our own ancestral lines, we bring healing to All Things.

## Chapter Eight - Becoming Self

There is an assumption that when we discuss anything spiritual, we're automatically referring to something beyond the body. One of the greatest omissions of New Age "wisdom" has been that of the body. We've heralded amazing techniques that teach us to be more mindful and guide us down our spiritual paths, but the body as innately spiritual has been overlooked, if not flat out denied and demonized.

We tend to separate approaches to wellbeing into Mind-Body-Soul, as if they are actually separate. We take care of the body (?), we feed it, we give it exercise, though we don't generally hold the perspective that the body *is* spiritual. We consider it the *vessel* holding what is spiritual.

The truth that New Age dogma hasn't thoroughly addressed is that the body is the constant through which we experience everything. Without its health, its neurotransmitters, its processing ability, and general faculties, what we intuit has no meaning, certainly no application. The body is more than the temple of the soul. It's the grounded celebration of its rapture.

Most of our mindfulness and ecstatic exercises to bolster the mind and soul lead us out of the body. And frankly, many masters of such techniques teach them as such, as if observing life beyond the body fixes everything. Ecstasy most definitely can expand our understanding of a great many things, though unless we can ground that information back into the vessel housing us, unless we can interpret that ecstatic trip in a way that better grounds our physical reality, trance isn't worth much.

The reality is, the body is Nature. It's wild, and it's already connected to All Things—that is, every living thing in Nature and beyond. Cosmology isn't out there. It's in our cells, and always has been. We don't have to journey out to get that. In fact, only ever journeying out is missing a vital component permanently residing within: the body doesn't have a relationship to the soul. The body *is* soul. The ability of our body to know this isn't broken. It didn't *fall*, it didn't disconnect. It's always been there. All we have to do is remember that fact. We have to learn to witness through it, and develop our unique system of understanding what its information is telling us.

My clients, Initiates, and students often joke about needing an owner's manual for being human, for getting through the human experience. In reality, that's what the body is. It's the perfect system of feedback for making our choices, discerning our truth, determining our health, the supportiveness of our environment—metaphorically and literally. How, then do we allow the body to become the divining rod? How do we become the fully sentient, between-worlds beings we were meant to be?

Most of us don't recognize when we're fully, deeply in our bodies. We don't know how to get there, and after much time spent detached from the body, being in it may not feel so heavenly. Maybe it's been hurt, and feeling embodied by the full self triggers emotional distress. Maybe we deal with chronic pain or other debilitating conditions that bring a charged understanding of what being in the body means. In such situations, being out-of-body is more comfortable. It's easier to float out, to dissociate and project our wisdom onto other entities—Spirit Guides, deities, Nature Spirits. We focus on intangible enlightenment such as learning our life purpose, honing our innate and intuitive skills, and helping others, yet we avoid seating into our own bodies to tend ourselves. What if none of the rest of that can come until we fully embody who we are?

Sometimes changing only a very small part of our ecstatic process produces dramatically altering results. Learning to go more deeply into the body's wisdom doesn't have to be any more detailed than that. For instance, take shapeshifting, a skill already known, one we all learn fairly early in shamanic education. Work with a skill we generally use to connect with an ally outside ourselves, and apply it to the body. We shapeshift into animals, trees, rocks, elements, plants... Shapeshift into self!

In a quiet space (preferably outdoors), eyes closed, alter the breath so that the inhale is more deep than usual, the exhale more prolonged. Stay with this style of breathing.

When breathing in this way is comfortable, bring the awareness to the sensations of being precisely in the immediate space. No daydreaming, no ticking tasks off the day list, no rabbit chasing. Stay in the immediate space. If the mind wanders off, just bring it back to deep breathing. It's okay.

Notice the effect of the atmosphere on the body. Is it cold/hot? Gentle/abrasive? It's okay that as the body's observation of the space clarifies, that the influence of Nature becomes more pronounced. In this state, the body is at home. It's natural for it to take in its surroundings.

Move as led. If a song comes up, sing it. Words need to be spoken? Utter them. Engage the elements as they support the body.

How does the body feel? Do sensations change as awareness lightens, seats? Do certain areas of the body respond differently, more intensely? Are they speaking? What do they say?

As awareness of the space and the body's interpretation of it sits deeper, ask the body to fully engage with the mind, the senses. Release thought. Whatever comes up, bless it, then let it go. Release programmed response, movement, utterance. The same way that we allow a strange animal, plant, element, or guide to shapeshift into our form, allow the body to take full command of every faculty offered.

Stay with this process of allowing only the body's dialogue. Interact with it as feels right.

When it feels appropriate, bring the focus back to breathing, and awareness back to the immediate space. Notice its sounds, temperature, sensations. Are they different than before? Is the experience of it the same?

Open the eyes, and observe who looks out of them.

Maybe each time we shapeshift into ourselves, the same sense of self comes. Perhaps a new one does. It doesn't matter, because we are infinite. The more we come into our body's experience of soul, the more we live no division, the more we learn the body as ancestor to everywhere we've been, we're prepared for everywhere we're going.

## Chapter Nine - Body as Intuition

We've talked about shapeshifting into ourselves to better step into our power. Taking that practice further, I'd like to talk about the many blessings and challenges of realizing the body's inherent spirituality.

Most modern shamanic circles focus on all things soul. They touch on amorphous inner world and philosophical cosmologies supporting the whole, though the experience of the form remains demoted in that hierarchy. I connect this oversight to a tendency for modern shamanists to avoid Middle World work, as they tend not to explore the spiritual nature of what is most immediately around us. Rather focus is on higher guidance, deeper resonance.

The more I root into being here, the more I realize the body is the portal. It has all the answers, and knows the questions we haven't thought to ask. We all get a body when we come into form, and it's pre-wired and ready to go for the most soul rocking experiences imaginable. The body is intuition manifest. It's the walking lexicon and interface of the spiritual map, all in one. It's how we are able to hear the mind, and the collection of a bazillion other senses that when we tune, remind us we're animals. We're Nature.

Yet we hit the ground running to dissociate from the body's wisdom. Ironically, the more we venture into spiritual community, often the less we incorporate the body's perspective. We meditate, we visualize, we get high—all things that in modern implementation serve to take us out rather than to root within. We don't often acknowledge that the body has a perspective, let alone many perspectives. And the idea that every cell has a story... Well.

Pain, or some degree of discomfort, is often the voice we're most willing to hear from the body. Again, it's ironic, because it's the one we least want to listen to. Because we live so outside the body's experience of form, the dialogue of pain presents a trove of information, expressing our experience as a world of hurt. That, we listen to.

How do we wear meatsuits, endure all the challenges doing so brings, and still remain connected with All Things? That's the challenge. Accomplishing that one thing sums the plight of being in form. There's no one way or right way to do it, and each of us has a unique job in realizing our personal tribulations in staying engaged. My challenge around these involves being a cyclic person, from which I derive my most profound power.

For the record, it has taken me about fourteen years to write that last sentence.

What's a cyclic person? Many things, the understanding of which is part of its unique challenge. Women identify with the phrase from the onset of menstruation. Certainly those who cope with fluctuating mood, mental health conditions, and chronic pain and fatigue relate. Men typically later in life comment around awareness of cycles, and how they affect their focus and energy.

For me, it's a combination of biochemical traits and chronic health conditions. I've never been diagnosed as having a mood 'disorder.' I have, however, been diagnosed with Polycystic Ovarian Syndrome (PCOS), Fibrymyalgia Syndrome (FMS) after a car crash in 2001, and have had minor strokes that among several outcomes, affected how I speak, read, and process data. While unofficial, my doctor approaches me on a spectrum of Premenstrual Dysphoric Disorder (PMDD). I work full-time. I maintain my writing career and my shamanic practice. I have a family, and a driving need to perform well at all of the above.

In the past, I've written about how having cyclic focus affects my ability to manifest the things I want. When focus shifts so frequently and has to be solely devoted to completing basic mundane tasks (ie getting through the day on no spoons), it can be hard to sustain the momentum needed for an ongoing spiritual discipline.

The bigger picture of my changing tides is that I work hard to fully encompass the many voices in my body. I talk to my body, emotions, and mind(s) as discrete beings, and I also hold dialogue with the conditions that I manage. I call FMS in as a spiritual entity and we talk by a stream in my Inner Garden. I frequently have tea with my neurotransmitters. I recently walked with my body to a mausoleum, where we released eras of sick relatives from my ancestral line. Likewise, when my mind just can't find a foothold in the reality that I want it to, I sit with it where it is. I keep it company, giving it what blessings I can, then I go to sleep, and wake to see where we've arrived, because I know it will be some place different.

Those moments that I just can't journey out and don't have the juice for high ritual, I put my energy into creative pursuit. Hands-on projects like artwork, gardening, and cooking go a long way for me to find the spiritual connections in the mundane and let them meet me. I don't always have to journey out to find allies or wisdom. They're very much available right in front of me, if I remember to stay open to them.

I've said often in articles, classes, and sessions, we can do all the soul work and healing we want. If the body's not in a place where the mind can accept it, spiritual healing can't stick. I'm willing to go all-in and say *it won't stick.*

Discern where the body is, really. What feels great about it, and what doesn't? Does it talk? Do we listen? I promise, the body is a prophet in disguise, and that disguise is the limitations amassed trauma has put on our beliefs of what our form can accomplish.

Get out the superhero cape. Put it on, and whirl around a few times. Ask the body what it most needs. Ask the conditions it manages how they inform, how they cradle, and how they alter perception of the ordinary.

Give up sick vocabulary, linear movement, and perceptions of how the form relates to the surrounding space. Through such effort, we can all become the brand new being we were when we got here, and see what it has always known, without impositions or corrections.

Shapeshift into the body as it is, now, however it feels. Allow it expression. Let it choose the sounds that come out, even if they make no sense. The less sense, the better! Give form the freedom to move the way it wants to, even if those ways feel odd. The movements that feel odd are the ones most heralding new territory. Nonlinear movement and sound are the ambassadors of rewiring the mind to the body's needs without ego interfering. Transform into the formlessness of deep being, and dive into what information lives there, because that is who we really are.

This observation isn't about learning the story of our body. It's about learning our body's story of ourselves, and those are not the same experiences.

## Chapter Ten – The Dream Team

When we focus on mundane support for skywalking seekers, resources at the fore are engaging reciprocity with Guides, becoming part of our own spiritual counsel, and finding etheric support in the life force around us. What about that of our immediate formed community, as in the people around us? How do they fit into our spiritual, if not animistic, Dream Team? How do we decide who should be on our Team?

For those who are new to the path of actively connecting with *aliveliness,* relying heavily on spiritual benefactors, as in Guides, Spirit Allies, or engaging totems in trance or in Nature is often the sum of the Dream Team. However profoundly those relationships impact our lives, we can't substitute them for human connection.

Of course, we can, but *should* we? Is it healthy to? Is it complete?

I'm open to arguments that we aren't all wired for the same kind of interpersonal connection. To clarify, I'm not talking about introversion versus extroversion. Rather, my emphasis is on deep, honest assessment about where humans fit into our animistic path. I meet so many animists who are deeply connected to, tend, and are tended by Nature, but care fuck-all about humanity. They want to save dolphins, though aren't motivated to meet their neighbors. Energetically, such a visceral disjunction in one area affects how we relate to every species. Everything is connected.

I freely admit, in the past I've dissed Camp Humanity, and since have realized what a self-defeatist, naïve victim stance such is. An assault on all is an assault on me, on us. As a result of compartmentalizing my compassion and awareness, I was faced with the limitations of my personal power from not being better connected to humanity, and the truth that my skills in deepening *any relationship* rely entirely on my intentional engagement in *every* relationship–animal, plant, element, human, discarnate... Of course, as we must become intimately aware of where we stand with humanity, we need to be vividly clear on what people we appeal to for help, and frankly, those to whom we do not.

How do we connect with people as spiritual allies? When in distress or need, most of us look to our partners or other loved ones for total support, only to wonder why the relationship implodes. First, one person can't hold everything, particularly if that support includes honoring expression around a deeply personal or traumatic event. Even if it's just the sharing of an experience outside that person's belief system or awareness, such a departure can create dissonance in the relationship. Second, just because our loved ones adore us and want to be supportive doesn't mean they're equipped to provide the depth of witnessing or assistance that we need, that which an objective, trained professional can provide.

And what if we don't find that trained professional? Many on the animistic path are dubious of working with caregivers in traditional modalities. We fear judgement, we fear change as much as anyone, and we often don't know who or what to look for, particularly in times of distress.

Along with those factors is inability to find the best-suited modality to meet our needs. Some of us of are land-locked, physically immobilized, socially isolated, and limited in available resources.

Maybe we don't communicate all that well and want that contact, despite feeling hindered in the interpersonal arena.

Further, sometimes it isn't personal help that we need, but education, information. Sometimes we just need to connect with someone who knows what we don't.

The people on the Dream Team don't have to be professionals. They can be listeners. Sometimes all we need is someone to witness our vision, our experience, our plans. We don't necessarily need feedback, reframing, or a nod, just a caring person. I've witnessed many seekers abandon a budding path because they didn't have anyone to talk to about their experiences. They didn't have a human community with whom they could share, seek guidance, find encouragement, sit in the woods, or overcome challenges. For such people, that lack of support eventually generates more stress in their lives than the experience that drove them out of the frame to begin with.

Like it or not, most of us need people as part of our spiritual path. We need the intimacy of sharing and creating space, exchanging experiences. Even the animal instincts to smell, feel, and hear the presence of others alters how we tread our soul travels. We also can't ignore each other as facets of our own healing, as mirrors and/or projections. We can't ignore where we as individuals become a collective.

Explore what interpersonal connectivity is most needed. What skills and personalities uplift? What ones limit? Why? It's just as important to be clear about what traits are needed, because mindlessly filling with relationships we don't need distracts us from connecting with those we do. Sometimes it's right not to engage, not because we cave to the fear of reaching out or trying something new, but because personal truth says, "Not this one. A better-suited relationship will come." Saying 'no,' goes a long way in finding right relationships.

To get a feel for who should be on the Dream Team, look around. Examine who's most often near. Do they fill life with delight? Do they challenge in affirming yet transformational ways? Do they drain? What does each individual bring to life that none other offers?

Explore ways to bless the people closest in life. Explore ways to affirm them. Consider letting go of unneeded relationships, and the most compassionate way to do so. Note areas in which human interconnection comes naturally, and those that could use some work.

In examining the people in everyday life, look at modalities of healing and learning. Consider the concepts of 'healing' and 'healer,' of 'learning' and 'teaching.' What modalities are implemented regularly? Do they fill needs? Have they become outmoded? What modalities are avoided? What ones incite curiosity? What is the best learning method or style? What educational approaches don't serve well?

Consider the following roles in examining human relationships and the personal spiritual path:

- Medical Doctor
- Acupuncturist
- Naturopath/Nutritionist
- Clergy
- Massage Therapist/Structural Integration Therapist
- Cognitive/Behavioral Therapist
- Witness/Listener
- Personal Trainer

- Legal Advisor
- Financial Advisor
- Teacher
- Shaman
- Energy Healer
- Horticulturist
- Artist
- People Like Ourselves
- People Different From Ourselves
- Friend
- Family
- Lover

These are but a few possibilities. Even if humans don't become a core facet of the animistic path, acknowledge that they are in some way significant to it. Make peace with how they fit into it. We have to challenge ourselves. Amongst those fetishes for animals and plants on our altars, the trinkets blessed by our Spirit Guides, we must insinuate some praise for our people–those we know, those we will never know, those we have let go. Honor the Dream Team, and it will find its way in blessing us.

## Chapter Eleven - Healing, Initiatory Crisis, and Community

*"We don't heal in isolation, but in community."*
*S. Kelley Harrell, Gift of the Dreamtime –*
*Reader's Companion*

In discussing personal and spiritual needs along the path of animist and shaman, community becomes intrinsically relevant. Whether undertaking to learn journeying, to fit for the role of shaman, or experience soul healing through any range of modalities, the number one contributing factor to pitfalls along that path that I see time and again is lack of community. I work with people for whom a class in journeying has cracked them down the middle without proper understanding of how to carry that changed perspective into regular life. I mentor people who want to serve as shamans, though function as the only animistic person in their familiar. I have sessions with clients who have had a healing session with someone else and have fallen into a funk, or they've had a session with me and leave elated, only to crash a few days or weeks later.

Each of these examples presents some form of initiatory crisis, or spiritual emergence. Initiation is the state of realizing that something needed isn't within grasp, or cannot coexist peacefully with the current status-quo. Initiatory crisis is stagnation characterized by distress in changing the status-quo. Every initiation reaches a point of crisis, by design. If it was easy to let go of the old way, there would be no need for initiation. We'd seat easily into new wisdom. We know that initiation has been completed when we allow status-quo to change and the new way of being to come in. Distress is relieved. The wisdom gained from this process is as valuable as the shift, itself.

Initiatory crisis that doesn't reach closure—ie, become wisdom—becomes PTSD, every time. In the case of feeling crisis after helpful ecstatic work or awe, distress increased. I could cite multiple reasons that the ecstasy ebbed. It may be due to lack of engaging personal spiritual discipline on a daily basis, or maybe a result of poor or total lack of mindfulness skills. Perhaps healing wasn't brought to its fullest potential, or deeper needs for healing were hidden. Maybe there's an undiscussed emotional or psychological imperative that occludes deep release. Fear may be dominant. There may be a lack of tools for how to deepen and ground spiritual emergence. I see each of these omissions often; however, the one downfall I see in almost every case of distress after ecstasy is a lack of community. People, in general, don't reach out for support. Worse still, they don't recognize the need to when it arises.

Some of this omission may be personal, but a good bit of it is collective, cultural, even. In the west, we're raised in an "I" culture. We're taught from birth to be self-reliant. If we're not capable of handling the bulk of life's challenges by ourselves, we're viewed as weak, failures. This message gets internalized to a profoundly damaging degree. Because we aren't taught a sense of collective reliance, accountability, responsibility, and joy, we don't recognize the signs that tell us we need such.

From a spiritual standpoint, the isolation created from the belief that we should be able to save ourselves sets us up for failure. Worse still, the idea that mere prayer and turning over our concerns and wounds to a higher power or Spirit Guides doesn't automatically alleviate us of them, engrains a sense of spiritual abandonment. "I gave it over; my need wasn't met. Now what?"

Without a cultural standard by which we recognize the symptoms of spiritual need, leaving the burden of communicating them on the person in crisis doesn't work, particularly if the person can't recognize that need for what it is. Often, people in crisis are so relieved—even blissful—at the time of the initial shift, they don't see the point of following up, of sustaining that healing momentum to revisit hallowed ground. Yet without a workable plan in place to support and sustain their initiation, they start to feel distress.

There are many reasons those in spiritual emergence don't seek further help. Foremost is that they don't recognize the signals telling them they need it. As far as we've come in our cultural dialogue of spiritual healing, the belief still persists that we can be miraculously cured of anything that ails us with one visit to the shaman, or one trip through our own ecstasy.

Maybe.

Sometimes.

Not really.

What is most common is a series of visits to the shaman, bolstered with support from other life areas between sessions and journeys. We wouldn't expect a broken leg to be healed in one visit to the doctor, supportive medication, physical therapy, yet we see subsequent returns to our spiritual workers as failure—on our part, the shaman's, the modality, the sacred space, our Guides, our Divinity, our attitude, the lighting...

And that's another thing. Because we divorce feelings and experiences into good/bad, welcomed/avoided, we have issues understanding why an amazing experience of awe can leave us profoundly sad. Ecstasy doesn't have to be frightening, heavy, or jarring to provoke a healing crisis. All it has to do is change us. *Leaving us so that we cannot return to our lives the same is enough to evoke absolute joy and fear, all in one sweep.* These states don't lie as polarities on a spectrum. They are conjoined in passion.

So we sink into feeling the ecstasy wasn't real. The shift must not have *really* worked. Shame sets in that healing couldn't be sustained. Fear of changing the mundane to support the awakening looms. Fear of being judged for awakening isolates. Guilt prevents getting further help. Each of these feelings and states are signals that a soul need is not being met. They are indicators that not only is ecstasy not being sustained, but by not taking it further, crisis is spiraling out of control. Under these circumstances, the initiation cannot be completed. When we can't see our own healing, our own initiations for what they are, we remove ourselves further from the possibility of being connected to community, thus to their resolution.

Even when we do recognize our healing and deeper need for community, it may not be possible to locate that tribe. Many people are socially or geographically isolated from others who share their spiritual path. They don't have people near them to connect with, or they're afraid to out themselves as a follower of a divergent belief system, or as someone uses alternative healing methods. Likewise, people fear not being able to afford community, whether that's an inability to pay for followup sessions/classes, give donations toward a drumming circle, or shoulder the responsibility of the interpersonal exchange that community requires.

What is community? In terms of initiatory crisis, what purpose does it serve? How does it influence healing? Who is community? The teacher or practitioner is part of the community and should be openly appealed to as such. Any spiritual leader who offers classes or sessions in soul healing should be available for what comes after. That said, teacher or healer doesn't form the whole of a community. S/he informs the drive to actively participate in one. The group that supports us needs to be people with whom we can speak openly, to whom we can listen steadfastly, and with whom we feel a close sense of belonging. It may be related to a shared spiritual belief or soul need. Tribe could be a group that only gathers for seasonal rituals. It could be a collection of individuals that don't know each other or form a group, proper, though each serves a need that shapes community for us. Perhaps this construct isn't ideal for some, though for others it could give collective support.

What is sometimes called the shamanic narrative, or healing story, is the tradition of healing through community. The idea that through sharing our story, we recognize commonalities, inspire, and evoke healing, creates the basis from which others gain the power to identify, share, and heal through their own stories.

We all love to be riveted by tantalizing tales. Our psychology has evolved to embrace and respond to them. When we listen to healing stories, they elicit neurological responses in us that drive empathy, compassion, and responsiveness. They inspire us to get up and do, to share our own story. I tell my story. Listeners begin telling theirs. In this way a single story heals a village.

That's the spiritual and neurological magick. The grounded function of community stems from something far more basic: the needs to be heard and to listen. Sometimes all we need is a witness. Other times we need input, tools, another modality, accountability, structure, empathy. We don't find these resources alone. Certainly, we may consult spirit guides and totems, though most people who are experiencing distress at a personal level also have problems making functional use of altered states. If we can't talk about our experiences, our experiences can't mature into a workable lifestyle that sustains healing and the completion of the initiation.

Consider what groups currently provide support. Do they support personal truth? Does personal truth even come up in the context of these groups? Are groups avoided? If so, be honest about the reasons why. How might community affect healing and spiritual growth? How might sharing the personal healing story affect someone else?

## Chapter Twelve - Embracing Community

It's an assumption that for animists, humans serving as part of our spiritual support community is an easy one. The perspective of animism assumes awareness of, if not connectivity with all souls. We comfortably project that view largely onto items we were domesticated to perceive as inanimate: trees, cars, rocks, clouds. Further, we're more at ease seeking soulful meetings with rattlesnakes than another person. Specifically, a lot of us are more at peace with solitary affinity, and avoid groups like the plague.

Not without good reason, of course. Most modern animists emerged from the church. We arrive back in the wild having chosen to leave an organized belief system that no longer works for us, and any structure that even remotely looks like it. However, when we make those kind of breaks, we realize in hindsight we're leaving more than a belief system.

Having grown up in a small community that revolved around a tiny country church, my family and church social engagements were inseparable. The same people I saw at Sunday services, choir practice, and youth group, were the same people I saw at Sunday lunch, the Saturday matinee, birthday parties, and holiday celebrations. They were the same people who gave my mom rides to work when the car broke down, had us over for cookouts, babysat me and my sister, and brought casseroles when there was a death in the family.

Despite however hypocritical, support is ingrained in the organized belief system; thus, when we leave the church, we leave such help behind. We're trained from an early age to believe that amenities are faith-based, so when faith changes aid disappears with the relationship. These mundane deal-breakers are like attempting to leave an abusive marriage. I've known congregation members to stay with a faith they don't believe in because they can't sustain without the material supports of the community. Ie, the community would disown them across the board, if they left. In times of need, there would be no one to call upon. Likewise, in times of joy, there would be no one to share them with.

The tangle of religion-of-birth and family can create incredibly painful interactions. Leaving the faith can alter families forever, particularly if those relationships were already strained. Again, some people never break from the church because they can't bear to lose family ties. Sometimes living soul interconnection out loud comes with strings, and we have hard compromises to make in extricating ourselves from the fraying loops. This emphasis on situational support grooms us to put spiritual needs after placating institutions, systems, and collective needs.

Many of us also haven't had good experiences with groups beyond church doors. Whether focused on earth-based spirituality, a specific cultural path, healing modality, soul practice, community interest, sport, or hobby, it isn't long before we realize the problems of organization affect every collective. At some point in development, every group has power struggles, personality clashes, imbalance of support, or a lack of necessary guidance. Such shadow dynamics are the human plight of meeting in numbers.

All of these experiences with groups shade our ability to connect collectively, as animists. When we allow such painful experiences to shape how we come together in groups now, we miss a vital component of personal growth. Don't misunderstand– there's certainly room for a healthy, progressive solitary path in any -ism. My concern for whether such isolation is truly working lies in how overall spiritual wellbeing continues to develop and grow. In most cases, it doesn't, not just due to going it alone, but from choosing to remain solitary out of fear.

The reason we go off-road isn't just rejection of the main path. It's also rejection of that base need to group with other humans, and denial of the necessary hoops we must jump in our personal development to deal with the trappings that come with being an active group participant. It's really no wonder that when I start talking about community to clients, Initiates, and students, their eyes glaze over, because they associate community with suffering. Their psyche folds under pressure from not being able to separate support from confinement, manipulation (perhaps even bullying), dogma, hierarchy.

How do we become animists or shamanists in isolation? How do we develop and maintain healthy boundaries between the personal part of our paths that can never be shared, and the part of our ever-conjoined paths that craves conscientious balance with others? We can't, until we honor how we arrived where we are.

The ability to find a group now rests solely on healing the wounds from joint interactions past. It's the healthy thing to do, but it's also the responsible soul thing to do. When we carry old wounds and try to engage with a group, we're ripe for having those wounds re-opened. For those of us who are particularly introverted, even the base dynamics of group interaction can send us recessing deeper into isolation. With such a reaction, though, isolation doesn't move us forward.

By facing social hurts of the past, we learn exactly what our boundaries are in new collective interactions. We come to intimately know what qualities make a good leader, contributor, witness, teacher, and supporter. As we make heart connections with these roles, we learn more about how to support ourselves and others. We internalize the very thing groups sought to teach us to start with: the true delineation lies in what needs we are required to fill ourselves, and the ones we need filled by others.

We don't have to give up the Nature community for a human one. In fact, culling our feelings about interpersonal networking to support our spiritual path can inform and strengthen all of our other connections. As with learning what needs should be filled by whom, we refine when to turn to which community.

I consider nature the First Tribe of us all. It's the community we fall deepest in love with as children, and one from which we draw a strong sense of wellbeing from a young age. For that reason, I always advise starting with Nature when reticent to rejoin the human community. The more we connect with Nature, the more we come to realize humanity is part of it. As humans aren't separate from nature, so we aren't separate from each other.

What needs does Nature fill at a personal level?

Consider how to give back to it.

What needs do people fill at a personal level?

Identify the current primary human communities.

Consider how to bless them.

## Chapter Thirteen - Go Deep or Lie

I spent much of 2015 in deep catharsis about what I'm doing on my path, what I want to do in my time on this planet. I've discussed it some in the *Betwixt* series, though it's largely remained a personal exploration.

Part of that curiosity has been sitting with realities around childhood dreams of making my living as a novelist tempered by the more practical results of publishing. My truth is that I never wanted to do anything else. Complicating that desire with the shamanic fury in my head has generated a deep sense of purpose for me. Yet like so many others who work the survival job and the passion job(s), I feel depleted and unable to make the strides I want in dazzling life areas because I expend so much energy just meeting mundane obligations.

The key to fusing elbow grease and manifestation is etheric relationship. I say it constantly to clients, Initiates, and students. Direct relationship is everything in animistic life. Anything desired must be connected with and embodied if it is to become. In other words, we must become it. We must shapeshift into it.

With that in mind, I recently ventured to call in the spiritual manifestation of Writing for a meeting of hearts. Instantly a lovely man in his mid-twenties came to my sacred space. His skin was metallic gold, and he was very fit.

I thanked him right away for having been with me, pretty much from my first awareness of love of writing in childhood. I thanked him for inspiration, stamina, imagination—the gamut of what it takes to truly take the ignited spark and light not just a page, but a book. In doing so, I felt deeply what it's like to have done just that, and to know that I will do it again.

Yet my heart grew sad around that thought, and I talked to him very openly about my disappointments, the changes in the industry, in my life, and how they have affected my desire to stick with it. I told him that while I love writing *Intentional Insights*, I didn't feel supported by the professional process, that it didn't give back nearly what it took out of me to create. He understood, and when I asked him what he needed from me, he stepped into my life force.

Being joined with him was familiar, invigorating in the same way as knowing what the next forty pages will say and racing to get the words out. As I experienced him conjoined with me, I became aware that connecting with Writing wasn't enough. I needed to connect with Publishing, too.

I wasn't thrilled about that. The writing isn't what sucks; it's the engine that is publishing, and how hard it is to retain visibility in the industry, even for established authors. As soon as I had the thought, an extremely tall man with the horns of an auroch appeared.

He glowed amber light and stood at least eight feet tall. His horns spanned ten feet easily.

He was a tad intimidating, though I proceeded to tell him my position on things. I spoke sincerely, as whine-free as possible, then waited. Without preamble, he stepped into me and Writing, and clear as day came the words, "Go deep, or lie."

*Embody, or fake it.*

*Honor, or complain.*

*Do, or shutup.*

*There's no between.*

The impact of his proclamation was such that I was temporarily thrown out of the trance. It happens. Sometimes what transpires in ecstasy is so profound that it can't be held, the moment can't be sustained. I breathed through the disruption and slowly made my way back to the space.

Upon becoming aware of them, I was again merged with both Writing and Publishing. I held that connection for as long as I could, sitting with the revelation of authenticity and how it relates to what I want in my time here. I let my imagination go as I experienced embodying the currents I want more of, and I recommitted to time with Writing and Publishing, regularly.

The other 'r' that travels with 'relationship' is reciprocity. Engagement goes two ways. It can't just be all about us and what we want from the connection or life. I often work with others who understand the relationship part, though don't engage reciprocity. They don't value the bond enough to see the other being in it, which while hard to do, is imperative in any relationship—interpersonal, or inter-spiritual.

When I asked Publishing what he needed from me, embodiment was his response. Expression. Acknowledgment.

The thing is, we have to woo what we want in life. We have to tell it it's pretty, buy it special things, make it feel spectacular. Modern Shaman and Podcaster, Christina Pratt, says a lot of profound things, though one gem she shared years back was the limitations of our intimate love relationships are mirrored in our etheric ecstatic relationships. Where we're afraid to go, or don't know how to proceed in intimate interpersonal bonds, we won't just magickally transcend in spirit work. It's not possible to go deeper in one part of life when we're not invested in others, because it's all related. That truth is at once transcendent and embarrassing, sad and liberating.

Who wants to admit their shortcomings in relationships? Who wants to truly overcome their personal shit to engage reciprocity? Yet nothing is gained without it.

Nothing is gained without it.

So, short of putting the cart before the horse—or the auroch in this case—my focus isn't on writing or publishing, but on the relationship with both as spiritual beings, and that of the other desires, people, I value most. My focus for now is on being in what I love, being in love with them, now.

Consider what's most wanted and how to create relationship with it. Is it possible to go deep with it, or continue sustaining the lie?

Is it possible to engage it in discussion, to learn what intimate reciprocity must manifest?

## Chapter Fourteen - The Truth about Sacred Space

I've spent many years expounding on the virtues of all land being sacred space. Every square inch of this planet is sacred. We have only to carry that awareness through every step we take. A few years ago, though, I had an experience that challenged my understanding of sacred space, and how we carry it with us.

In 1998, I went to Ireland. It's no big secret that I've always felt a spiritual draw to the culture and land of Eire. However, visiting it in journey and *actually* being there were two different things. Not only were my precious etheric ties to the land deepened while I visited, they were substantiated in a way that created deep crisis in my life.

While there, I unexpectedly experienced what I can only describe as a time fold, of being the me that I am in this life having the experience of modern Ireland, alongside the experience of another me from an Ireland, past. Through that experience, I came to know my first birthplace into form was in the area of Powerscourt Fall. The realization left me deeply shaken, and I wasn't entirely sure why.

Even sites on that trip without etheric personal connection were lively. I had very clear indications one step to the next that the land in one spot is not the land—in another spot. On one patch of land I'd feel electricity jolt through my body, liveliness, fire. On another right next to it, I'd find cool watery streams bathing my cells. It was as if these places were stations along radio bandwidth and I was the tuner giving them expression.

Several places functioned like natural pads for trance postures. I'd stand on a spot and hear voices, which stopped as soon as I stepped away. Others seemed to open portals to unseen spaces, in which I heard music. Some places that spoke to my body were collective sacred sites like Newgrange and Tara, while others were run-of-the-mill pastures filled with bleating sheep. Regardless, the places that spoke to me were replete with clear indication that I wasn't the only human to come along and feel that keen liveliness, and in feeling the energy of those places, I could feel the legacy of other people who'd also intuited them, perhaps even made use of them.

As amazing as those experiences were, they challenged my philosophy that all space is sacred. I knew in my heart it was true, though I couldn't rationalize why some spots seemed "more sacred" than others. I was forced to own that some places feel different, which as an *amongst* animist, challenged me at a deep level. Despite realizing that we all sense things differently and we sense different things, I was blown away by the fact that while all land is sacred, it's not enlivened in a similar way. Sacred space that just is felt very different from space I created for rituals, classes, healing sessions. It wasn't the same, and I needed to clarity around that.

To further confuse the issue, throughout life I'd had experiences of very disturbed land, what some may refer to as cursed areas. I'd met trees hundreds of years old that completely, intentionally disregarded humanity, and did not take serious my offer to cultivate relationship with them. Other places hosted energy gateways, pores in the land, which built-up life force passed through healthily. Other such pores had fouled in some way, and stagnant life force became shadow that hosted rampant crime and desecration of the land. I couldn't understand how all land was sacred, yet such variation existed in its function and state.

Before we moved into our home several years ago, we took every opportunity to form relationship with the Nature Spirits there. Among them were spirits of the trees, mineral spring, and Land Elders—human spirits, who in death chose to stay as sentinels of the land. The first night I slept there, I woke to find a man standing at the foot of my bed. Under the bright moonlight, I could see that his skin was mocha, and his long dark hair was pulled back into two long tails with strips of cloth binding them every few inches, scalp to end. He was dressed in a long skin shirt that hung loosely over skin pants. A leather pouch was bound to his middle. He told me that he was a Land Elder, and he was there to work with me when I was ready.

Though I engaged the Nature Spirits of our place and thought of the Land Elder often, it was a couple of years before we formed a close relationship. The more time I spent with the Land Elder, I realized that all land supporting humans requires the humans living on it to be spiritual conduits. Every being living on a piece of land, whether raccoon, yew tree, or granite deposit, must consciously pay into the etheric web of that land, like a spiritual homeowner's association. This collective body functioned as a council of living and spiritual keepers united to assure that the wellbeing of all inhabitants was tended, thoroughly.

A few years later I began a formal seidr study. I'd been drawn to the runes and Old Norse traditions since my late teens, and having settled well into my local Nature Spirits I felt secure in committing to study a cosmology sourcing from a different land. As I began it, though, I noticed a shift in the relationship of my home Nature Spirits.

When I asked them about it, they asked me why I was reaching back in time to study a dead pantheon. They wanted to know why I was tapping into the Nature Spirits of a far away land, instead of finding deeper relationship with them.

I was stunned. I'm a Druid with a lifelong, rich relationship with trees. I asked my Nature Spirits, "Why, if all trees talk to each other, does it matter where in the world I am, and what spiritual paths I study?"

"It doesn't," they responded.

Clearly things had been disrupted, and I wanted to understand the rift.

After much angst on my part, they told me again, that every human-inhabited patch of land requires inter-relationship with a human, and that was all they would say.

I carried this question for several months, into my seidr working, taking every opportunity to hold space with local Nature Spirits. Nothing clarified.

Some time later, I was invited to do work in Boone, North Carolina. It wasn't the first time I'd done sacred work there, and I'd long realized the unique life force of the mountains, compared to other places I'd worked. Particularly, the life force of the cove where I worked, is always very charged. I jokingly call it 'living on the positive end of a battery,' which isn't far from the truth. In the decade plus that I've traveled there, I've never slept soundly through a single night. The atmosphere is so enthusiastically alive that I have an extremely hard time bringing my mind and body to rest, yet am oddly refreshed, despite that.

This particular time, as I called in the directions, to my astonishment they were already there. I thought those exact words as I completed my opening ritual, and felt silly. Of course they were already there. All land is sacred. Yet, something about the dynamic and moment was completely different.

I went through the work I was required to do, then when I was alone again, I sat with the Nature Spirits of the area. What came of that profound interaction answered questions I'd had about sacred space since returning from Ireland in 1998.

All land is sacred, but it's a little like a tree falling in the woods. Sure, it's still sacred even if there's no human to observe it. We carry with us the anthro-centric skill of making anything sacred to suit our rituals, our ceremonies, as we intend it. Have intention, sacred will travel. However, the longterm spiritual needs of the land can't be met without human interaction, simply because of the fact that we're on the planet, and we're powerhouses of growth, as well as destruction. We must be actively engaged with the land, not just tenants on it. Because Nature went on before us and it will go on after us doesn't remove us from being a part of the full picture. Nature Spirits need the human element as much as we need them.

What I learned in that moment was that places in which the spiritual human-to-Nature relationship has been actively sustained are easier to connect with, as in Boone and parts of Ireland. In those places, the directions are a tad closer upon calling them. The elements lean a smidge nearer when summoned, and the Elders readily communicate what the land needs. There's no hazing to make sure humans are onboard, because in that place, the relationship has been actively maintained.

The communication between wights and humans is already well-translated into terms humans can understand; thus, they can readily act. Without that reciprocal relationship, the land becomes depleted and unhealthy. Gateways weaken and become corrupted due to the long-lacking relationship. When the land gets sick, humans become ill and disconnected collectively, and personally.

Given that significance alone, this connection is a good reason for why ancient and indigenous shamans stuck to their own bioregion to form relationships with their land—to keep the areas healthy at all levels, to keep the sacredness of their space continuous, sustaining. Every one of us can't tend every speck of the planet, though we can compassionately represent the human element for the one that we occupy, the one that claims us.

This wisdom is what my Nature Spirits were trying to impress upon me. I can venture into the cosmology of any path I want, as long as I remain the human in etheric concert with them. Their question wasn't for me to answer to them, but to myself. The roots of one place connect into the roots of all places. Remembering that perpetual connection makes travel and staying put ever sacred.

So go outside and mark a spot. Start reaching out, and hold self open for the wights that stretch back. It may take some time and a few precious offerings, but the offer will be met.

It will be met.

## Chapter Fifteen - Deathwalking Midgard

Mid-January 2016, something happened that I was reticent to openly discuss. I talk about a lot of things In the Betwixt Series, and most of them are uncomfortable at best. This one, though, left me unsettled, and even more adrift at the thought of bringing it to others.

As I was driving down the road, I heard a voice. That's not an unusual occurrence. I've had otherly takeovers before, whilst driving—particularly one noted in my book, *Real Wyrd*. And if I'm completely honest, I've experienced times of spirit possession before, but this was something else, completely.

For starters, it was spontaneous. I was driving home on the first gorgeous day we'd had since November. The sky was perfect cerulean blue, not a cloud, glimmering sunlight, when suddenly I heard a voice in my head. Not unusual, though this one wasn't one I often hear, by which I mean hadn't heard it in years. Spokesperson for a group of higher beings I refer to as the Light Council (to others the White Brotherhood, Aesir, Enochian beings, etc.) it spoke so rapid fire, the only way I could understand it was to say the words aloud, along with it. As soon as I did, the voice that came from my mouth wasn't mine, and I couldn't control the words. They were, "We can't stop it. There's nothing we can do."

This went on for some time, and the only reason it ceased is because I became self-conscious with an abrupt, "WTFZOMGS!" I was totally discombobulated and bawling, and for a few lingering seconds felt overwhelming sadness, guilt, and disappointment. I also knew without doubt I was experiencing the feelings of this being, and it was referring to Earth.

*As in, the planet.*

*As in, what humans have done here can't be reversed, and we need to own that.*

*As in, some strata of gods can no longer hold back the effects of what we've done, and have had to admit defeat.*

*As in, hospice, for a planet.*

*As in, deathwalking is needed, now.*

Before I concur with how crazytown it sounds, I'd like to discuss some interesting patterns I've witnessed last few years. Much of it is UPG (unverified personal gnosis), derived from personal work and others I've worked whose spiritual paths I've supported and facilitated for almost twenty years.

I've seen a lot of shit. But mostly what I've seen is a lot of *the same shit*; meaning, for years, not much changed. Well, it's changing, now, and it isn't stopping.

I offer that the majority of my clients, Initiates, and students since mid-2012 have expressed a lack of ability to find center. However, when we work more deeply, it isn't that center can't be found; rather, it's that center keeps moving.

Those of us who have been on the renegade spiritual path for a long while, usually as practitioners of some avenue of it, have enjoyed years of functional tactics, appropriate responses to shifting inner scapes that provide what's needed. Since that same timeframe, many colleagues have shared with me that their tried methods for personal balance don't work anymore, and the ones that bring results work short-term, a day, maybe a week. They've whispered dismay and embarrassment, as if they've lost their mojo, can't be healed, can't heal. In reality, it's nothing they're doing or not doing.

In fact, empaths that they are, the terminal state of Nature is expressing itself through them.

Cosmologies that have provided wisdom and discipline for decades suddenly are foreign. In the shorter term, by the time elements are called into sacred space, they've shifted. The space releases itself. It moves on without us.

In that timeframe, I've also had perfectly sound people tell me they can't control their own minds and feelings. Moods and states of being come upon them as if they aren't their own, generating crises that feel foreign.

Inexplicable anger, grief, anxiety, and sadness, rise as in the depths of mourning.

Because when a planet can't find stasis, neither can anything that lives on it. Without is within.

Since October of 2015, I've worked with several people for whom the Elders of their land are leaving or have left. In truth, my relationship with my own has been strained, of late. In fact, they have recently left this realm, which has put me in the new position of Land Elder of my region.

That shift in Land Elders is the point that I realized just how pivotal the current planetary shift is. We've made base assumptions about life on Earth since we got here. In truth, they've been solid assumptions--things like, the sun will always rise, most definitely in the east, always setting in the west, north will always be north, south will be south, land boundaries are fixed. Yet, we know that's not true. Our sun has an expiration, which means we do, too. The poles have shifted before, it's just not in our cellular memory. And land that we've inhabited since our dawn is no longer habitable. Even our waterways are changing.

And on the more esoteric plane, we assume the Nature Spirits will always be connected to the land, to the elements. We take for granted that the Land Elders will always tend their end of the bridge, balanced by an engaged human on the other end. The reality is, the lack of human engagement on that passage in many regions, the destruction of the land, itself, has created an energetic imbalance we can't fix. Many of our Land Elders have left, and no human is stepping up in their stead.

These things are not just in flux, they have changed. Even the sun's position with regard to the earthly vantage point is contested. Try to throw a rock and hit a season. Confidantes who are astute sky readers and weather oracles and have set their guidance by Nature, herself, find their lexicons shifting and scarcely legible for the first time in decades--if ever.

The last few years have been nothing but constant shifts, with time flying. And we know this. Somewhere deep down in our cells, we know our time living carte blanche on Midgard, Gaia, however we know Her, is limited, and somewhere in the Dreaming, an expiration has been surpassed. Who knows when, how, or what it means. I don't, though I know we have hit a point of no return. The message I was given doesn't mean stop saving endangered species and rainforests. It means change the intention of Earth stewardship from one of fixing what can't be fixed to midwifing it all to What Comes Next, whatever that is. It means continuing to try to stop what has come to pass creates conflict with giving Her a dignified passage. It means it's time for us all to start doing what we do best, all day, every day, and own it as our gift from the Multiverse, and the gift we give with every breath.

Does it all end? Do we end? Do we have a decade or a thousand? I don't know. I know that words can't express the relief I felt that the turmoil of the last few years finally made sense, that as the ultrasensates we are, we have been feeling Her demise without realizing it. We've sounded Her fear, Her disillusionment through our own emotions. Whatever comes, we are Her, and can't resist the call to grow into Her next phase of being, any more than we can resist our own.

Consider personal calling to serve the planet. How might that service manifest in the mundane? In etheric work? How does serving the planet create intimate connection with every being on it? Beyond it?

# Praise for Gift of the Dreamtime

Harrell draws you into the dreamtime as an expert novelist draws you into a great novel and shares with you her experiences and knowledge of the world beyond the veil from the time she was very young. ~ *Innerchange Magazine*

In this book that hunger and fear that nibbled and clawed at you and me for years is explained in poetic, experiential detail. Kelley guides us into our own souls, turning the "whys" into wise. ~ Bridgett Walther, author of *Conquer the Cosmos*

Let S. Kelley Harrell guide you on a very special spiritual journey — destination your healed soul! ~ Donna Henes, author of *The Queen of My Self*

Absolutely recommend *Gift of the Dreamtime* to anyone, especially those working to overcome their own traumas. *~Facing North*

Kelley Harrell acts as a guide to help us move from deep trauma to wisdom. A brave book, beautifully insightful, that leads us to greater knowing of ourselves. ~ Gail Wood, author of *The Shamanic Witch*

*Gift of the Dreamtime* gives hope for those of us who sometimes feel we're not doing things right, or that perhaps there is no healing to be had. *~Pagan Book Reviews*

# Praise for Teen Spirit Guide to Modern Shamanism

Teen Spirit Guide to Modern Shamanism is a brilliant book! Kelley Harrell provides you with a wealth of tools to assist you in cultivating your own shamanic path. This is an important book to help readers create a life filled with depth and meaning. Great guide! --Sandra Ingerman MA, *Soul Retrieval* and *Shamanic Journeying: A Beginner Guide.*

I can think of no better book for a young person to read to inform themselves of the essentials, acquire techniques that will fill the yearning, and begin on their journey. Teen Spirit Guide to Modern Shamanism is highly recommended, not just for teens and young people, but for anyone beginning to explore shamanism. --June Kent, Editor of *Indie Shaman Magazine*

This book is responding to the simple fact that children are already in the Middle World. They're already having experiences, and into their teens and as young adults, they're looking for answers for how to do something with it, in how to train it, how to discipline it. This book is genius. --Christina Pratt, *An Encyclopedia of Shamanism*

# Ancient Healing, Modern Shamanism

## www.soulintentarts.com

Follow Kelley at:

https://www.facebook.com/soulintentarts

https://www.instagram.com/kelleysoularts

@kelleysoularts

Read Kelley's open dialogue with souls, Intentional Insights, The Weekly Rune, Life Betwixt, and learn more about The Spirited Path Modern Shamanism and Reclaiming the Runes Intensives at Soul Intent Arts

www.ingramcontent.com/pod-product-compliance
Lightning Source LLC
Chambersburg PA
CBHW032020090426
42741CB00006B/674